planet earth

GROWING READER
LEVEL 3
700-1500 WORDS

WILD AMAZON

by Lisa L. Ryan-Herndon

SCHOLASTIC INC.

New York   Toronto   London   Auckland   Sydney
Mexico City   New Delhi   Hong Kong   Buenos Aires

BBC (word mark and logo) are trade marks of the British Broadcasting Corporation and are used under licence.
Planet Earth logo © BBC 2006. BBC logo © BBC 1996.
Love Earth logo™ BBC.
Published by Scholastic Inc. SCHOLASTIC and associated logos are trademarks and/or registered trademarks of Scholastic Inc.
Lexile is a registered trademark of MetaMetrics, Inc.
Cover design by Michael Massen. Interior design by Michael Massen and Aruna Goldstein.
ISBN-13: 978-0-545-10128-8
ISBN-10: 0-545-10128-X

12 11 10 9 8 7 6 5 4   9 10 11 12 13 14/0

Printed in the U.S.A.
Printed on paper containing minimum of 30% post-consumer fiber.
First printing, March 2009

This book travels into the Amazon,
a mysterious place where hundreds of
thousands of different species live.
Scientists believe thousands
are yet to be discovered!

Storms in the Sahara Desert blow sand across the world to fertilize the Amazon rainforest.

A spectacular river and the world's largest rainforest form the amazing place called Amazonia or, the Amazon. At 1.2 billion acres, Amazonia spreads across nine countries in South America covering 25 percent of the continent.

Plants, animals, and people need water to survive. Rivers provide us with drinkable water, food, transportation, and energy power. The Amazon River carries 20 percent of the world's flowing water.

This river starts its 4,000-mile-long journey in the Andes of Peru, the world's longest mountain range. The Amazon River twists eastward across the South American continent and empties at the coastline of Brazil, into the Atlantic Ocean.

PIRARUCU

The pirarucu's lunglike organ helps it breathe air during the low-water season.

More than 3,300 species of fish swim in the Amazon River. Some grow to extraordinary sizes in these waters that are rich with food. The pirarucu, also called the arapaima, is the longest freshwater fish in South America, measuring more than eight feet long and weighing up to 300 pounds!

In South America, the dorado catfish swims 3,000 miles upstream—from the river's delta to the Andean foothills—in the longest migration of any freshwater fish. Packed with so many fish, the river can look like it's boiling.

DORADO CATFISH

GREEN ANACONDA

During the high-water season, the Amazon River swells, creating the swamps where the world's heaviest snake hunts for food. The green anaconda, a member of the boa constrictor family, averages 300 pounds in weight and up to 20 feet in body length. Its diet ranges from fish to crocodiles—anything it can catch, squeeze, and swallow.

The boto, or pink river dolphin, is the largest freshwater dolphin species in the Amazon River. It can grow more than eight feet long, and weigh up to 220 pounds. Botos use echolocation to follow the dorado catfish through the river's muddy waters. Botos work together to herd the fish into shallower waters, where its long beak with 35 pairs of teeth is perfect for scooping up meals!

The boto's smaller cousin, the tucuxi or estuarine dolphin, is five feet long and weighs about 100 pounds. These timid little dolphins are unusual: they are found in both salt and fresh water. Tucuxi resemble smaller versions of the bottlenose dolphin, with a longer beak and a hooked dorsal fin. Unlike botos, the tucuxi dolphins stay in the lake areas when the rivers flood to avoid becoming landlocked.

Electric eels live in the deepest waters of the Amazon. They have weak eyesight, so they send out 10-volt charges to sense what's around them, just as dolphins use echolocation. Don't touch! At five feet long, electric eels carry a charge of 600 volts—enough to knock out a human.

The rarest mammal in the Amazon is the giant river otter. This three-foot-long, 70-pound otter builds nests in the lake areas where it lives with its family. Giant river otters are nicknamed

"wolves of the river" because they hunt in packs of up to nine members.

GIANT RIVER OTTER

Although tropical rainforests cover only three percent of the Earth's surface, these habitats are the powerhouses of our planet. One third of all plant and animal species live inside the Amazon, the world's largest rainforest.

Every species plays an important role in this ecosystem. With little wind, flowers and fruits need bugs and birds to spread seeds throughout the forest. Fungi have the important role of breaking down dead plant and animal matter on the forest floor, returning nutrients to the soil.

BULLET ANT

One acre of land can be home to three million ants.

About 80 percent of all insects live in rainforests. Ants are the most plentiful of predators. At one inch long, the bullet ant is very large with huge jaws, or mandibles, that it uses for biting, fighting, and carrying things. It is named for its fiery sting—the pain can last up to 24 hours!

With so many ants, what more could a tree-climbing anteater want? Using its 15-inch-long tongue, this mammal slurps up ants, termites, bees, and honey. This anteater, also known as the southern tamandua, is six feet long and can weigh up to 15 pounds. It hangs from tree branches by its 20-inch-long tail, and pokes open nests with its sharp claws.

TREE-CLIMBING ANTEATER

JAGUAR

Jaguars will hunt in water.

The largest cat in the Americas is always looking for a meal. The jaguar grows up to six feet long and can weigh up to 350 pounds. This predator eats whatever it can catch, from fish to monkeys. Its jaws are so powerful it can crack a turtle's shell. Little is known about this cat because it hunts and lives alone.

Plenty of heat and food make it easy for the world's largest spider to grow as big as a dinner plate. The goliath bird-eating spider earned its name with a 10-inch leg span and a diet of snakes, bugs, mice, and birds caught by its poisonous fangs.

GOLIATH BIRD-

GLIDING LEAF FROG

High in the trees, the gliding leaf frog sings at night. Time to fly — webbed feet and skin folds help this amphibian jump between trees, gliding up to 50 feet. This frog can grow up to three inches long on a strict diet of bugs.

This rainforest bird loves leaves—for eating. Plants are a heavy meal and don't digest easily. The hoatzin waits for the special bacteria in its digestive system to break down the leaves. This process can take two days and the nasty smell earned the hoatzin its nickname, stinkbird.

HOATZIN

A fig tree is the place to be. In just one day, 44 species of birds and monkeys can come to the branches to feed on the figs.

Sharing this tasty fruit is not easy.

SPIDER MONKEY

First in line is the spider monkey. With its large brain and long arms, this monkey finds the ripe fig tree fast and early. One arm swings the spider monkey 40 feet between trees. This monkey is smart enough to swing away from a fight when the next group shows up.

Emperor tamarins also eat flowers, bugs, eggs, and frogs.

Groups of between 3 to 15 emperor tamarins race across the fig tree's branches on all four limbs. At only nine inches tall, these monkeys are too small to fight, so they eat and run when the next group of monkeys climb up for a meal.

EMPEROR

SQUIRREL MONKEY

The squirrel monkey likes to get its meals to go. Like the emperor tamarin, it can't stand up to its bigger cousins, even with more than 10 family members in the same tree. It is best to pick up a meal and get out before the bullies start yelling.

The capuchin monkey is the loudmouthed bully of the monkey kingdom. Smart and brave, they chatter and shout, throw sticks, and pull the tails of any animal in their way!

This monkey gets its name from its famous noisy yell, which males make to tell the other groups where the troops are currently

feeding. This helps them save energy as they can avoid patrolling a territory and conflicting with other monkeys.

Just like in the fig tree, there are a limited amount of resources to be shared among many species. Sharing isn't easy, but by working together, we can all enjoy our extraordinary world. Remember the Three R's: Reduce. Reuse. Recycle. These are important ways to cut down on consumption and waste.

We all live on Planet Earth

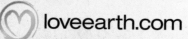 loveearth.com